FOCUS on FRACTIONS

Revised

1

By Margaret A. Smart
Patricia A. Tuel

FOREWORD

FOCUS ON FRACTIONS is a series of three carefully sequenced booklets for students in grades five to nine. The series is designed to give the student a successful experience in fractions and stresses increasing his computational ability through success oriented experiences.

Book 1 develops concepts using groups, regions, and number lines. Book 2 helps the student understand and practice addition and subtraction. Book 3 presents multiplication and division of fractions using pictures and developing rules. Each book contains five quizzes which should be given after the appropriate review page. Puzzle pages for fun and practice are part of each book.

The series can be used as part of an individualized program or as a whole class activity. The booklets were written so that the student can work on his own with minimum teacher assistance.

The authors recommend the use of manipulative materials such as *FRACTION TILES* with the program.

This is the third edition of *FOCUS ON FRACTIONS.* The books were typeset on the Macintosh Computer by Margaret A. Smart.

Mary Laycock
Mathematics Specialist
Nueva Learning Center
Hillsborough, California 94010

Copyright 1977
(Third Edition 1986)
Activity Resources Company, Inc.
P.O. Box 4875
Hayward, California 94540

FOCUS ON FRACTIONS
BOOK 1

FRACTION CONCEPTS

Margaret A. Smart & Patricia A. Tuel

CONTENTS

EQUAL PARTS OF A WHOLE

A fraction is an equal part of a whole thing. Take a picture like this.

Divide it into two equal parts.

Shade in one of the parts and you have a picture of 1/2.

Use a ruler to divide each of the pictures below into two equal parts. Shade 1/2 of each picture..

Focus on Fractions, Book 1 © 1977, 1987 Activity Resources Co., Inc. PO Box 4875, Hayward, CA 94540

EQUAL PARTS OF A WHOLE

The picture below has been divided into four equal parts. Each part is one of four equal parts or 1/4.

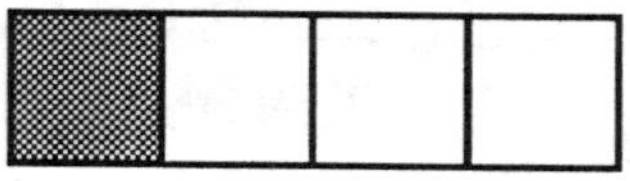

Shade 1/4 of these pictures.

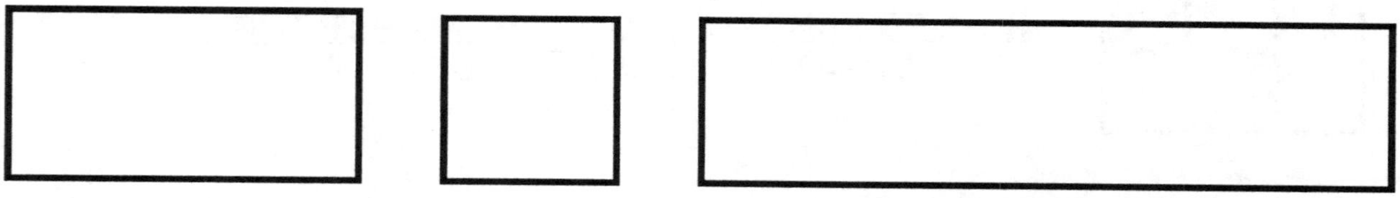

The picture below has been divided into three equal parts. Each part is one of three equal parts or 1/3.

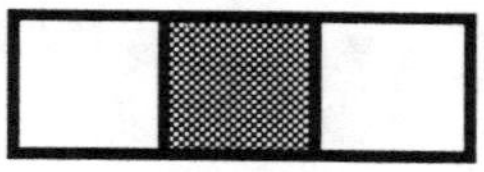

Shade in 1/3 of each of these pictures.

Write a fraction for the shaded part of these pictures.

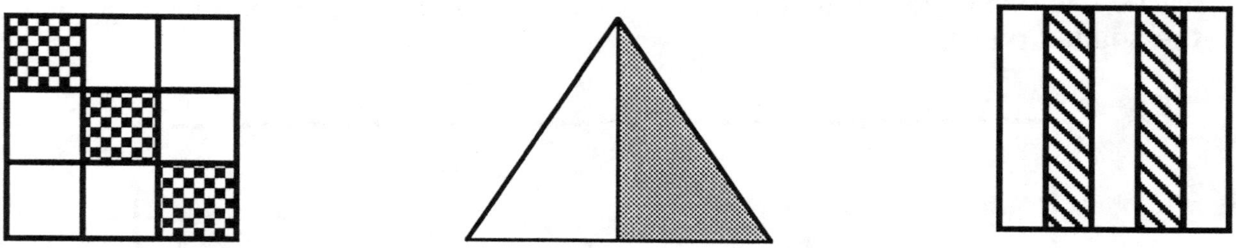

___   ___   ___

Focus on Fractions, Book 1 © 1977, 1987 Activity Resources Co., Inc. PO Box 4875, Hayward, CA 94540

NUMERATOR AND DENOMINATOR

Every fraction has a top and a bottom number. The top number is called the
NUMERATOR and the bottom is called the DENOMINATOR.

$$\underline{2} \quad \textbf{NUMERATOR}$$
$$3 \quad \textbf{DENOMINATOR}$$

Examples:

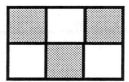

$$\frac{\underline{\text{SHADED PARTS}}}{\text{TOTAL PARTS}} = \frac{3}{6} = \frac{\text{NUMERATOR}}{\text{DENOMINATOR}}$$

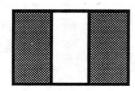

$$\frac{\underline{\text{SHADED PARTS}}}{\text{TOTAL PARTS}} = \frac{2}{3} = \frac{\text{NUMERATOR}}{\text{DENOMINATOR}}$$

Try these:

          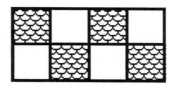   

___   ___   ___

Divide this rectangle into 6 equal parts. Shade in 4 parts. Write the fraction for
the shaded part.

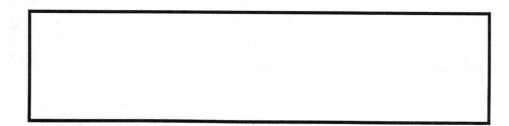

Focus on Fractions, Book 1 © 1977, 1987 Activity Resources Co., Inc. PO Box 4875, Hayward, CA 94540

WRITING FRACTIONAL NAMES

THE DENOMINATOR TELLS YOU THE NUMBER OF PARTS INTO WHICH THE WHOLE HAS BEEN DIVIDED.
THE NUMERATOR TELLS YOU THE NUMBER OF THOSE PARTS THAT YOU ARE CONSIDERING.

In the fraction $\frac{2}{3}$, the numerator is _____.

In the fraction $\frac{2}{3}$, the denominator is _____.

In the fraction $\frac{7}{8}$, the 7 is called the _____.

In the fraction $\frac{7}{8}$, the 8 is called the _____.

Write a fraction with a numerator of 5 and a denominator of 7_____.

Write a fraction with a denominator of 9 and a numerator of 5_____.

The denominator is the (top,bottom) number of a fraction _____.

The numerator is the (top, bottom) number of a fraction _____.

Fill in.

$\frac{5}{10}$ name is five-tenths.

$\frac{3}{5}$ name is three-fifths.

$\frac{6}{7}$ name is _____-sevenths.

$\frac{1}{6}$ name is _____-sixth.

$\frac{4}{8}$ name is _____-eighths.

$\frac{5}{12}$ name is _____ - _____.

$\frac{1}{4}$ name is _____ - _____.

$\frac{9}{10}$ name is _____ - _____.

$\frac{3}{8}$ name is _____ - _____.

Focus on Fractions, Book 1 © 1977, 1987 Activity Resources Co., Inc. PO Box 4875, Hayward, CA 94540

FRACTION PUZZLE

In the spaces below, write the letter that represents the shaded part of each figure.

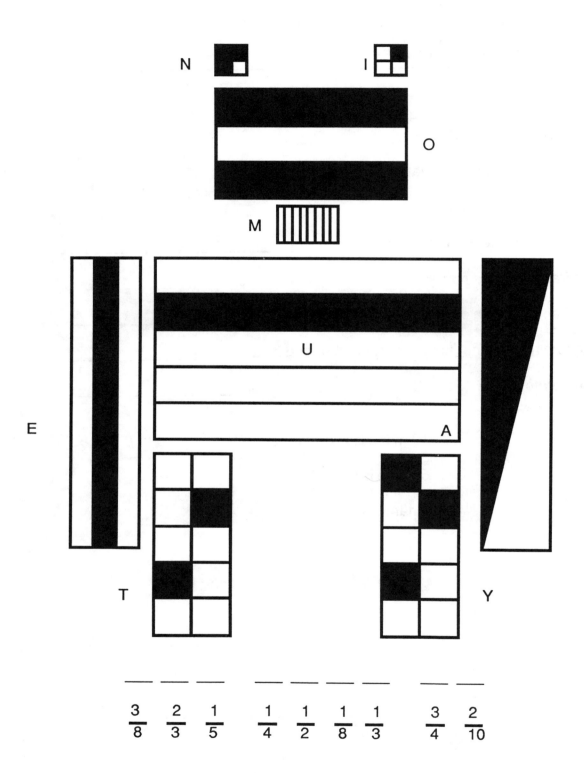

$$\frac{3}{8} \quad \frac{2}{3} \quad \frac{1}{5} \qquad \frac{1}{4} \quad \frac{1}{2} \quad \frac{1}{8} \quad \frac{1}{3} \qquad \frac{3}{4} \quad \frac{2}{10}$$

EQUAL PARTS OF A GROUP

A fraction can mean an equal part of a group.

Take a group like this.

Divide it into two equal groups.

Shade in one of the groups.
You have a picture of 1/2.

Divide each group below into two equal parts. Shade 1/2 of each group.

EQUAL PARTS OF A GROUP

This group has been divided into four equal parts. Each part is 1/4 of the group.

Divide each of the groups below into four equal parts. Shade 1/4 of each group.

The group below has been divided into three equal parts. Each part is 1/3 of the group.

Divide each of the groups below into three equal parts. Shade 1/3 of each group.

Shade 1/5.

Shade 1/6.

Shade 1/8

Focus on Fractions, Book 1 © 1977, 1987 Activity Resources Co., Inc. PO Box 4875, Hayward, CA 94540

MORE WORK WITH GROUPS

THE DENOMINATOR TELLS YOU THE NUMBER OF PARTS INTO WHICH THE GROUP HAS BEEN DIVIDED.

THE NUMERATOR TELLS YOU THE NUMBER OF THOSE PARTS THAT YOU ARE CONSIDERING.

EXAMPLE:

$$\frac{\text{SHADED PARTS}}{\text{TOTAL PARTS}} \quad \frac{2}{3}$$

Divide into thirds. Shade 2/3.

Divide into halves. Shade 1/2.

Divide into fifths. Shade 3/5.

Divide into fourths. Shade 3/4.

Divide into sixths. Shade 2/6.

Divide into sevenths. Shade 1/7.

Focus on Fractions, Book 1 © 1977, 1987 Activity Resources Co., Inc. PO Box 4875, Hayward, CA 94540

FRACTIONS ON THE NUMBER LINE

This is a picture of a segment of a number line.

The segment has been divided into 4 equal parts.

The arrow shows 1/4.

The arrow shows 2/4.

Draw an arrow to show 3/4.

Divide the segment below into 2 equal parts. Show 1/2 with an arrow.

Divide the segment below into 3 equal parts. Show 2/3 with an arrow.

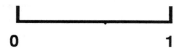

Divide the seqment below into 8 equal parts. Show 5/8 with an arrow.

Write the fractions indicated by the arrows.

Focus on Fractions, Book 1 © 1977, 1987 Activity Resources Co., Inc. PO Box 4875, Hayward, CA 94540

LET'S REVIEW

A fraction is an equal part of a _____ thing.

Write a fraction for the shaded part of each picture.

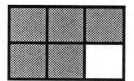   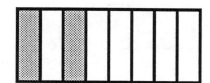   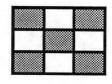

——   ——   ——

Write the numerators of the following fractions.

3/4   7/8   9/16   4/5   15/16   2/3

——   ——   ——   ——   ——   ——

Write the denominators of the following fractions.

3/4   7/8   9/16   4/5   15/16   2/3

——   ——   ——   ——   ——   ——

Circle 4/5 of this group.   Circle 3/4 of this group.

Write the fraction indicated by the arrows on each number line.

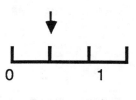

(Take Quiz 1)

Focus on Fractions, Book 1 © 1977, 1987 Activity Resources Co., Inc. PO Box 4875, Hayward, CA 94540

MATCH UP PUZZLE

Each fraction name can be matched with a fraction picture and a number line. Connect the dots from each fraction name to the correct fraction picture and then to the correct number line.

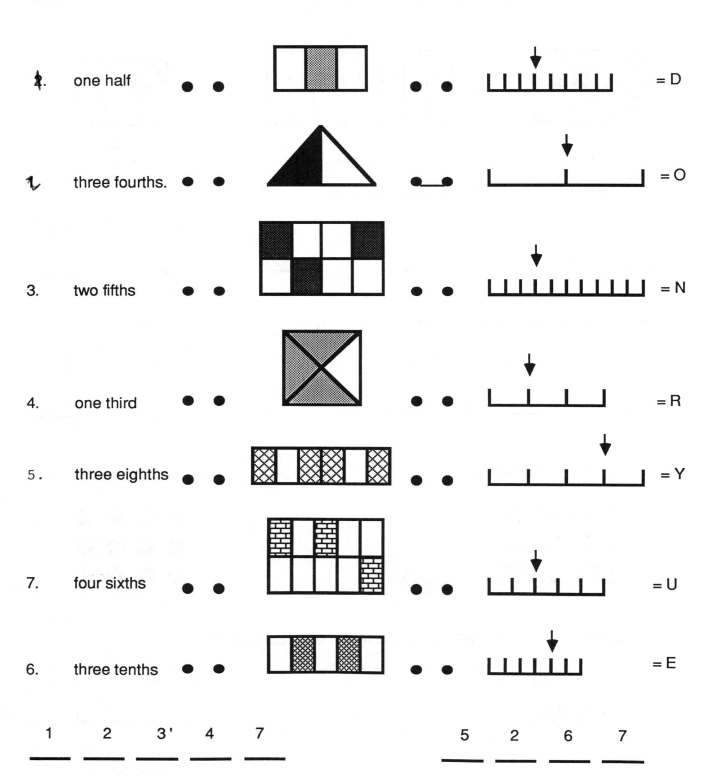

one half	= D
three fourths.	= O
two fifths	= N
one third	= R
three eighths	= Y
four sixths	= U
three tenths	= E

1   2   3'   4   7   5   2   6   7

___ ___ ___ ___ ___   ___ ___ ___ ___

Focus on Fractions, Book 1 © 1977, 1987 Activity Resources Co., Inc. PO Box 4875, Hayward, CA 94540

COMPARING FRACTIONS

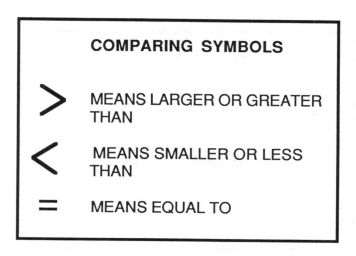

COMPARING SYMBOLS

> MEANS LARGER OR GREATER THAN

< MEANS SMALLER OR LESS THAN

= MEANS EQUAL TO

Use the symbols in the chart to compare the first fraction picture with the second.

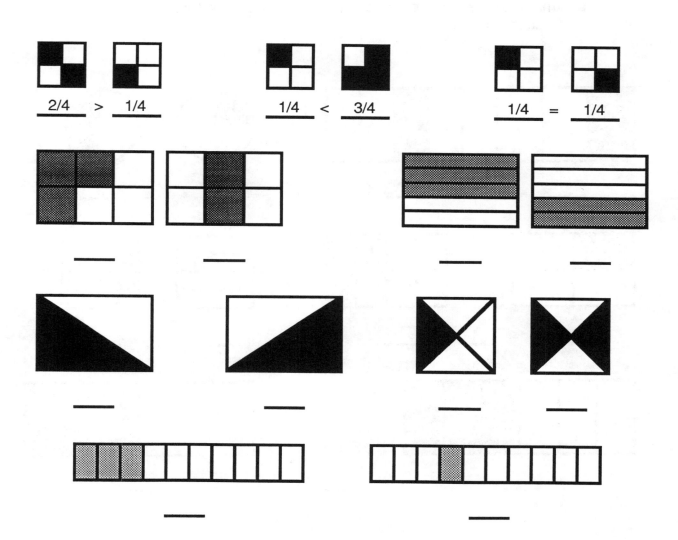

2/4 > 1/4   1/4 < 3/4   1/4 = 1/4

Focus on Fractions, Book 1 © 1977, 1987 Activity Resources Co., Inc. PO Box 4875, Hayward, CA 94540

COMPARING FRACTIONS

Use the symbols in the chart to compare the first fraction picture with the second. Write the fraction below each picture.

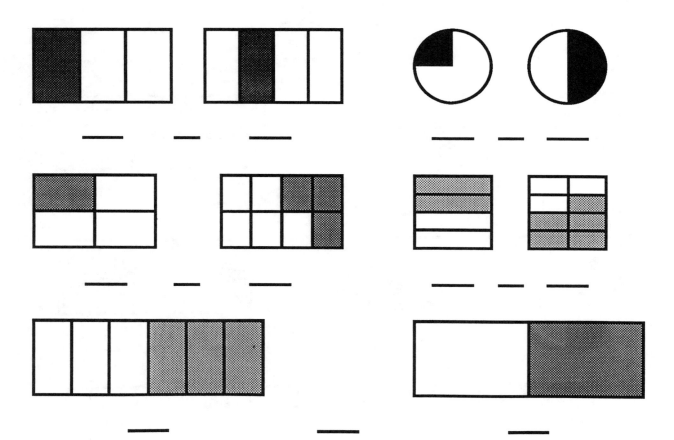

Focus on Fractions, Book 1 © 1977, 1987 Activity Resources Co., Inc. PO Box 4875, Hayward, CA 94540

PUZZLE PAGE

Arrange the fraction pictures in order from smallest to largest to spell a word.

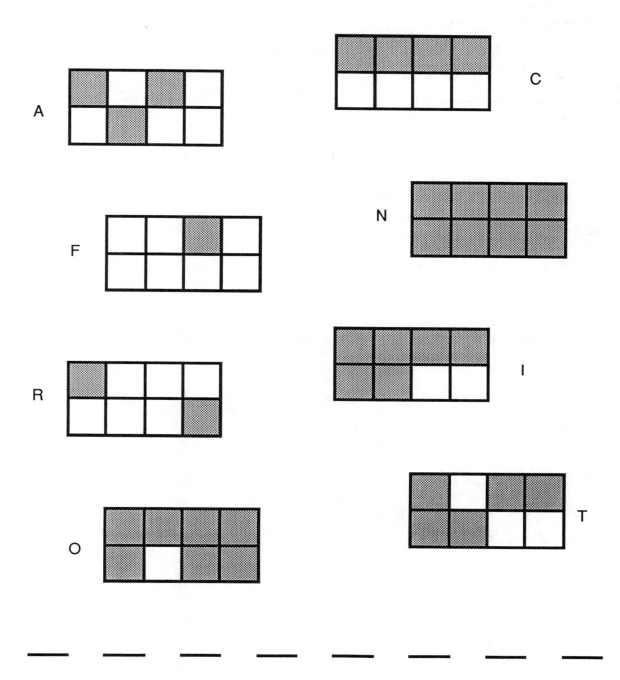

_____ _____ _____ _____ _____ _____ _____ _____

Focus on Fractions, Book 1 © 1977, 1987 Activity Resources Co., Inc. PO Box 4875, Hayward, CA 94540

FINDING EQUIVALENT FRACTIONS

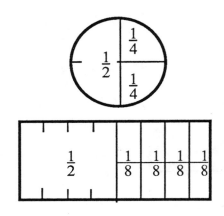

1/2 of the circle is equal to 2/4 of it.

1/2 and 2/4 are equivalent fractions.

They name the same thing.

1/2 of the rectangle is equal to 4/8 of it.

1/2 and 4/8 are equivalent fractions.

To find equivalent fractions, we will multiply the numerator and the denominator of a fraction by the same number.

Examples:

$$\frac{1}{2} \times \left(\frac{2}{2}\right) = \frac{2}{4} \qquad \frac{1}{2} \times \left(\frac{3}{3}\right) = \frac{3}{6} \qquad \frac{1}{2} \times \left(\frac{4}{4}\right) = \frac{4}{8}$$

Write in the circle the number that you must multiply by to make the fractions equivalent.

$$\frac{1}{2} \times \left(\frac{5}{5}\right) = \frac{5}{10} \qquad \frac{1}{2} \times \left(\ \underline{\ \ }\ \right) = \frac{7}{14} \qquad \frac{1}{2} \times \left(\ \underline{\ \ }\ \right) = \frac{9}{18}$$

$$\frac{1}{3} \times \left(\ \underline{\ \ }\ \right) = \frac{2}{6} \qquad \frac{1}{3} \times \left(\ \underline{\ \ }\ \right) = \frac{3}{9} \qquad \frac{1}{3} \times \left(\ \underline{\ \ }\ \right) = \frac{5}{15}$$

$$\frac{1}{4} \times \left(\ \underline{\ \ }\ \right) = \frac{3}{12} \qquad \frac{1}{4} \times \left(\ \underline{\ \ }\ \right) = \frac{5}{20} \qquad \frac{1}{4} \times \left(\ \underline{\ \ }\ \right) = \frac{8}{32}$$

Focus on Fractions, Book 1 © 1977, 1987 Activity Resources Co., Inc. PO Box 4875, Hayward, CA 94540

FINDING EQUIVALENT FRACTIONS

$\dfrac{3}{5} = \dfrac{}{10}$ What times 5 is 10? $5 \times 2 = 10$.

$\dfrac{3}{5} \times \left(\dfrac{2}{2}\right) = \dfrac{}{10}$ Multiply the numerator and the denominator by 2. $\dfrac{3}{5} \times \left(\dfrac{2}{2}\right) = \dfrac{6}{10}$

Try these.

$\dfrac{3}{5} \times \left(\dfrac{6}{6}\right) = \dfrac{}{30}$ $\dfrac{1}{6} \times \left(\dfrac{7}{7}\right) = \dfrac{}{42}$ $\dfrac{2}{3} \times \left(\dfrac{8}{8}\right) = \dfrac{}{24}$

$\dfrac{5}{10} \times \left(\dfrac{2}{2}\right) = \dfrac{}{20}$ $\dfrac{1}{9} \times \left(\dfrac{-}{}\right) = \dfrac{}{36}$ $\dfrac{2}{7} \times \left(\dfrac{-}{}\right) = \dfrac{}{35}$

$\dfrac{3}{8} \times \dfrac{}{} = \dfrac{}{16}$ $\dfrac{4}{5} \times \dfrac{}{} = \dfrac{}{25}$ $\dfrac{1}{2} \times \dfrac{}{} = \dfrac{}{20}$

$\dfrac{3}{4} \times \dfrac{}{} = \dfrac{}{12}$ $\dfrac{5}{8} \times \dfrac{}{} = \dfrac{}{16}$ $\dfrac{3}{16} \times \dfrac{}{} = \dfrac{}{32}$

Show how you would find the missing numerators.

$\dfrac{2}{8} = \dfrac{}{24}$ $\dfrac{2}{3} = \dfrac{}{15}$ $\dfrac{5}{6} = \dfrac{}{36}$

$\dfrac{1}{2} = \dfrac{}{14}$ $\dfrac{7}{12} = \dfrac{}{36}$ $\dfrac{2}{3} = \dfrac{}{18}$

Focus on Fractions, Book 1 © 1977, 1987 Activity Resources Co., Inc. PO Box 4875, Hayward, CA 94540

MAKING A TABLE OF EQUIVALENT FRACTIONS

Look for a pattern in each row and fill in the spaces.

TABLE OF EQUIVALENT FRACTIONS

1/2	2/4	3/6	4/8	5/10	6/12	7/14	8/16
1/3	2/6	3/9	4/12	5/15	6/__	7/__	8/__
2/3	4/6	6/9	__/12	__/15	__/__	__/__	__/__
1/4	2/8	3/12	__/__	__/__	__/__	__/__	__/__
3/4	6/8	9/12	__/__	__/__	__/__	__/__	__/__
1/5	2/10	3/15	__/__	__/__	__/__	__/__	__/__
2/5	4/10	6/15	__/__	__/__	__/__	__/__	__/__
3/5	6/10	9/15	__/__	__/__	__/__	__/__	__/__
1/6	2/12	3/18	__/__	__/__	__/__	__/__	__/__
5/6	10/12	15/18	__/__	__/__	__/__	__/__	__/__

Focus on Fractions, Book 1 © 1977, 1987 Activity Resources Co., Inc. PO Box 4875, Hayward, CA 94540

LET'S REVIEW

Write the fraction indicated by the arrow on each number line below.

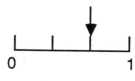

_____   _____

Use the symbols < or > to compare the first fraction picture with the second.

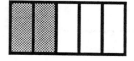   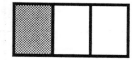   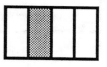   

_____   _____

Insert the missing numerator or denominator so that each pair of fractions will be equivalent.

$\frac{2}{3} = \frac{6}{}$ $\frac{1}{4} = \frac{}{12}$ $\frac{2}{5} = \frac{10}{}$ $\frac{4}{7} = \frac{16}{}$ $\frac{2}{27} = \frac{}{81}$

$\frac{3}{8} = \frac{21}{}$ $\frac{5}{6} = \frac{}{48}$ $\frac{4}{5} = \frac{20}{}$ $\frac{2}{7} = \frac{14}{}$ $\frac{1}{7} = \frac{11}{}$

$\frac{10}{12} = \frac{30}{}$ $\frac{11}{12} = \frac{}{48}$ $\frac{9}{9} = \frac{81}{}$ $\frac{5}{7} = \frac{}{35}$ $\frac{4}{9} = \frac{28}{}$

Circle the pairs of fractions that are <u>not</u> equivalent.

$\frac{1}{2} = \frac{5}{10}$ $\frac{1}{3} = \frac{15}{21}$ $\frac{3}{4} = \frac{16}{20}$ $\frac{5}{9} = \frac{17}{27}$ $\frac{3}{8} = \frac{12}{32}$

$\frac{4}{9} = \frac{22}{45}$ $\frac{6}{7} = \frac{48}{56}$ $\frac{5}{6} = \frac{23}{30}$ $\frac{3}{8} = \frac{15}{40}$ $\frac{2}{8} = \frac{12}{32}$

$\frac{19}{20} = \frac{18}{19}$ $\frac{10}{12} = \frac{50}{60}$ $\frac{8}{9} = \frac{36}{45}$ $\frac{6}{7} = \frac{44}{49}$ $\frac{3}{5} = \frac{28}{45}$

(Take Quiz 2)

Focus on Fractions, Book 1 © 1977, 1987 Activity Resources Co., Inc. PO Box 4875, Hayward, CA 94540

PUZZLE PAGE

2 = A	6 = E	14 = G	21 = H
20 = L	42 = M	3 = O	8 = R
33 = S	24 = T	4 = U	5 = Y

Solve each equivalent fraction below. Find the letter that represents each of the missing numerators or denominators in the chart and write it in the correct space.

$$\frac{1}{2} = \frac{5}{10} \qquad \frac{1}{3} = \frac{\underline{}}{9} \qquad \frac{1}{4} = \frac{\underline{}}{16} \qquad\qquad \frac{1}{6} = \frac{\underline{}}{12} \qquad \frac{2}{3} = \frac{\underline{}}{12} \qquad \frac{3}{4} = \frac{\underline{}}{8}$$

$$\frac{1}{7} = \frac{\underline{}}{14} \qquad \frac{4}{9} = \frac{\underline{}}{45} \qquad \frac{6}{7} = \frac{\underline{}}{49} \qquad \frac{1}{4} = \frac{\underline{}}{12} \qquad \frac{9}{11} = \frac{27}{\underline{}} \qquad \frac{3}{7} = \frac{\underline{}}{56}$$

$$\frac{2}{3} = \frac{\underline{}}{36} \qquad \frac{2}{7} = \frac{6}{\underline{}} \qquad \frac{4}{7} = \frac{\underline{}}{14} \qquad \frac{1}{15} = \frac{\underline{}}{45} \qquad \frac{1}{2} = \frac{2}{\underline{}} \qquad \frac{2}{5} = \frac{\underline{}}{35} \qquad \frac{1}{7} = \frac{3}{\underline{}}$$

LOWER AND HIGHER TERMS

> **THE NUMERATOR AND THE DENOMINATOR OF A FRACTION ARE CALLED ITS TERMS.**
>
> $\frac{1}{2}$ $\underline{\text{NUMERATOR}}$ TERMS
>   DENOMINATOR

This is a set of equivalent fractions for 1/2.

1/2	2/4	3/6	4/8	5/10	6/12	7/14	8/16

Circle 4/8 in the set above. Compare the other fractions in the set with 4/8.

       1/2,   2/4,   ____   all have lower terms than 4/8.

5/10,   6/12,   ____   ____   have higher terms than 4/8.

Write the lower and higher terms of the fraction that is circled in each set below.

SETS OF EQUIVALENT FRACTIONS	LOWER TERMS	HIGHER TERMS
1/2 2/4 3/6 4/8 (5/10) 6/12	1/2 2/4 3/6 4/8	6/2
1/4 2/8 3/12 (4/16) 5/20 6/24	_____	_____
2/5 4/10 6/15 8/20 (10/25) 12/30	_____	_____

Focus on Fractions, Book 1 © 1977, 1987 Activity Resources Co., Inc. PO Box 4875, Hayward, CA 94540

REDUCING FRACTIONS TO LOWER TERMS

TO REDUCE FRACTIONS TO LOWER TERMS, DIVIDE THE NUMERATORS AND DENOMINATORS BY THE SAME NUMBER.

EXAMPLES:

$\dfrac{2}{4}$ can be reduced if you divide the numerator and the denominator by 2.

$$\frac{2}{4} \quad \div \quad \boxed{\frac{2}{2}} \quad = \frac{1}{2}$$

$\dfrac{3}{9}$ can be reduced if you divide the numerator and denominator by 3.

$$\frac{3}{9} \quad \div \quad \boxed{\frac{3}{3}} \quad = \frac{1}{3}$$

Reduce these fractions to lowest terms by dividing the numerators and the denominators by the number shown in the box.

$$\frac{4}{8} \div \boxed{\frac{4}{4}} = \underline{\quad}$$
$$\frac{9}{12} \div \boxed{\frac{3}{3}} = \underline{\quad}$$
$$\frac{10}{15} \div \boxed{\frac{5}{5}} = \underline{\quad}$$

$$\frac{2}{6} \div \boxed{\frac{2}{2}} = \underline{\quad}$$
$$\frac{12}{32} \div \boxed{\frac{4}{4}} = \underline{\quad}$$
$$\frac{4}{12} \div \boxed{\frac{2}{2}} = \underline{\quad}$$

$$\frac{12}{18} \div \boxed{\frac{3}{3}} = \underline{\quad}$$
$$\frac{4}{6} \div \boxed{\frac{2}{2}} = \underline{\quad}$$
$$\frac{7}{21} \div \boxed{\frac{7}{7}} = \underline{\quad}$$

$$\frac{6}{18} \div \boxed{\frac{3}{3}} = \underline{\quad}$$
$$\frac{10}{30} \div \boxed{\frac{5}{5}} = \underline{\quad}$$
$$\frac{12}{24} \div \boxed{\frac{6}{6}} = \underline{\quad}$$

REDUCING FRACTIONS TO LOWEST TERMS

A FRACTION IS IN LOWEST TERMS
IF IT CANNOT BE REDUCED.

Here is an example pf a fraction that has been reduced to **lower terms**. It must be reduced again to **lowest terms** by dividing once more.

$$\frac{6}{12} \div \boxed{\frac{3}{3}} = \frac{2}{4} \qquad \frac{2}{4} \qquad \text{is not in lowest terms.}$$
$$\text{Divide again.}$$

$$\frac{2}{4} \div \boxed{\frac{2}{2}} = \frac{1}{2} \qquad \frac{1}{2} \qquad \text{is in lowest terms.}$$

Always try to divide the numerator and the denominator by the largest number possible when you are reducing a fraction.

Reduce these fractions to **lowest terms**. Remember to divide the numerators and the denominators by the **same** number.

$$\frac{5}{10} \div \boxed{\frac{5}{5}} = \frac{1}{2} \qquad\qquad \frac{6}{12} \div \boxed{} = \text{—} \qquad\qquad \frac{4}{16} \div \boxed{} = \text{—}$$

$$\frac{6}{8} \div \frac{\text{—}}{\text{—}} = \text{—} \qquad\qquad \frac{9}{18} \div \frac{\text{—}}{\text{—}} = \text{—} \qquad\qquad \frac{2}{16} \div \frac{\text{—}}{\text{—}} = \text{—}$$

$$\frac{4}{6} \div \frac{\text{—}}{\text{—}} = \text{—} \qquad\qquad \frac{8}{12} \div \frac{\text{—}}{\text{—}} = \text{—} \qquad\qquad \frac{9}{27} \div \frac{\text{—}}{\text{—}} = \text{—}$$

$$\frac{12}{36} \div \frac{\text{—}}{\text{—}} = \text{—} \qquad\qquad \frac{9}{36} \div \frac{\text{—}}{\text{—}} = \text{—} \qquad\qquad \frac{8}{20} \div \frac{\text{—}}{\text{—}} = \text{—}$$

$$\frac{12}{32} \div \frac{\text{—}}{\text{—}} = \text{—} \qquad\qquad \frac{9}{15} \div \frac{\text{—}}{\text{—}} = \text{—} \qquad\qquad \frac{10}{25} \div \frac{\text{—}}{\text{—}} = \text{—}$$

Focus on Fractions, Book 1 © 1977, 1987 Activity Resources Co., Inc. PO Box 4875, Hayward, CA 94540

LET'S REVIEW

EQUIVALENT FRACTIONS

Write the next three fractions in each set.

$\dfrac{2}{3}$ $\dfrac{4}{6}$ $\dfrac{6}{9}$ $\dfrac{8}{12}$ ___   ___   ___

$\dfrac{2}{7}$ $\dfrac{4}{14}$ $\dfrac{6}{21}$ $\dfrac{8}{28}$ ___   ___   ___

$\dfrac{3}{5}$ $\dfrac{6}{10}$ $\dfrac{9}{15}$ $\dfrac{12}{20}$ ___   ___   ___

HIGHER TERMS

Change these fractions to higher terms.

$\dfrac{3}{4} = \dfrac{\quad}{12}$ $\dfrac{5}{8} = \dfrac{\quad}{16}$ $\dfrac{2}{3} = \dfrac{\quad}{18}$ $\dfrac{2}{3} = \dfrac{\quad}{9}$

$\dfrac{5}{6} = \dfrac{\quad}{36}$ $\dfrac{6}{7} = \dfrac{\quad}{21}$ $\dfrac{3}{16} = \dfrac{\quad}{32}$ $\dfrac{3}{5} = \dfrac{\quad}{40}$

$\dfrac{1}{2} = \dfrac{4}{\quad}$ $\dfrac{2}{3} = \dfrac{6}{\quad}$ $\dfrac{3}{4} = \dfrac{12}{\quad}$ $\dfrac{2}{5} = \dfrac{8}{\quad}$

LOWEST TERMS

Reduce these fractions to lowest terms.

$\dfrac{2}{4} = $ ___ $\dfrac{3}{9} = $ ___ $\dfrac{2}{16} = $ ___ $\dfrac{2}{12} = $ ___

$\dfrac{3}{15} = $ ___ $\dfrac{2}{20} = $ ___ $\dfrac{4}{24} = $ ___ $\dfrac{10}{16} = $ ___

$\dfrac{10}{25} = $ ___ $\dfrac{9}{12} = $ ___ $\dfrac{6}{9} = $ ___ $\dfrac{3}{30} = $ ___

(Take Quiz 3)

Focus on Fractions, Book 1 © 1977, 1987 Activity Resources Co., Inc. PO Box 4875, Hayward, CA 94540

FRACTION PUZZLE

Shade in each fraction that is in lowest terms.

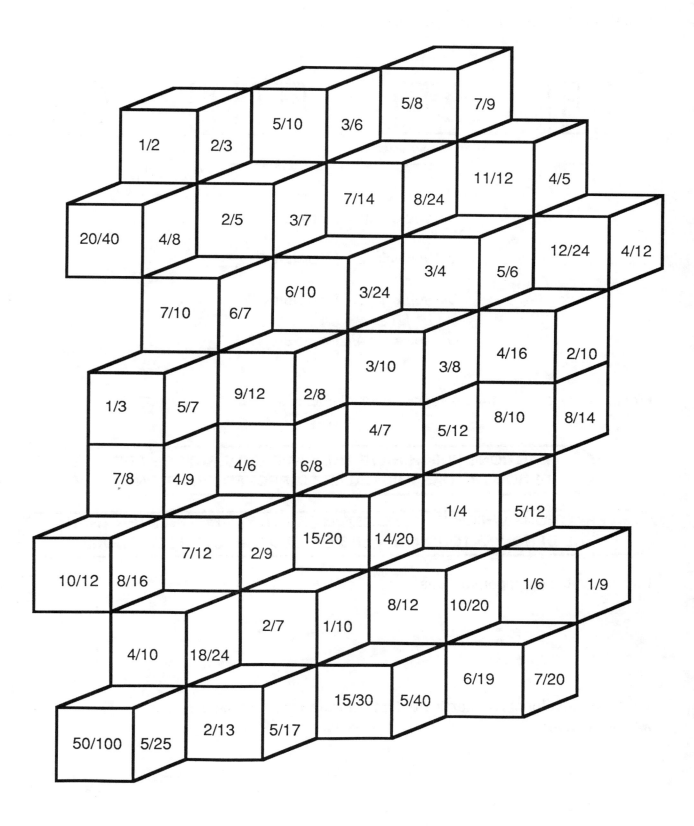

Focus on Fractions, Book 1 © 1977, 1987 Activity Resources Co., Inc. PO Box 4875, Hayward, CA 94540

IMPROPER FRACTIONS

Write a fraction for the shaded part of each picture.

1.

2.

3.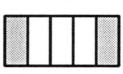

4.

——   ——   ——   ——

Did you write 1/4 for picture 1? ____

Did you write 2/2 for picture 2? ____

Did you write 2/5 for picture 3? ____

Did you write 4/4 for picture 4? ____

Fractions like 2/2 and 4/4 are special kinds of fractions.

> **FRACTIONS WHICH HAVE THE SAME NUMERATORS AND DENOMINATORS ARE CALLED IMPROPER FRACTIONS.**

> **FRACTIONS WHICH HAVE NUMERATORS THAT ARE GREATER THAN THE DENOMINATORS ARE ALSO CALLED IMPROPER FRACTIONS.**

Circle all of the improper fractions.

$$\frac{8}{5} \qquad \frac{3}{8} \qquad \frac{9}{4} \qquad \frac{6}{3} \qquad \frac{2}{7} \qquad \frac{9}{9} \qquad \frac{7}{7}$$

Write a numerator or a denominator for the following so that each fraction will be improper.

$$\underline{11} \qquad \underline{47} \qquad \underline{10} \qquad \underline{13} \qquad \frac{\underline{}}{12} \qquad \underline{23} \qquad \frac{\underline{}}{16}$$

Focus on Fractions, Book 1 © 1977, 1987 Activity Resources Co., Inc. PO Box 4875, Hayward, CA 94540

MIXED NUMBER AND IMPROPER FRACTIONS

> A MIXED NUMBER IS A WHOLE NUMBER PLUS A FRACTION.
> EXAMPLES: 1 1/4   2 1/2   5 3/5

Circle all of the mixed numbers.

1/8   5 3/4   4/9   4 7/8   2/5   6 2/3   1/2

Here are some pictures of mixed numbers.

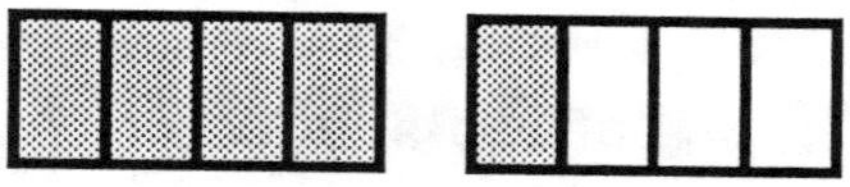

Each picture has been divided into _____. How many fourths are shaded? _____.

We can write an improper fraction of 5/4 or a mixed number of 1   1/4.

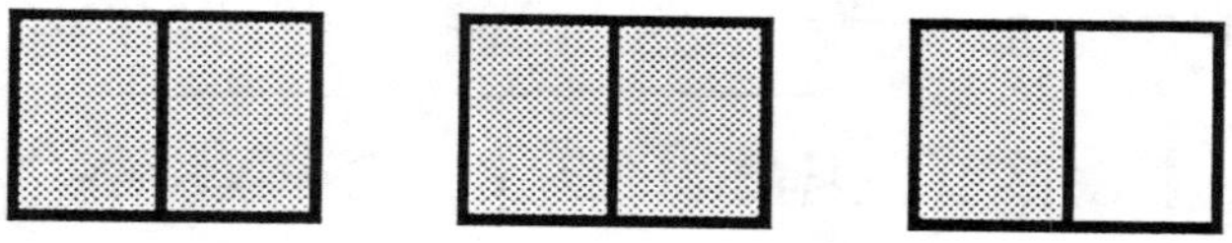

Each picture has been divided into _____. How many halves are shaded? _____.

We can write an improper fraction of _____ or a mixed number of _____.

Divide each picture below into thirds. Shade in the correct number of thirds to show the mixed number 3   1/3 and the improper fraction 10/3.

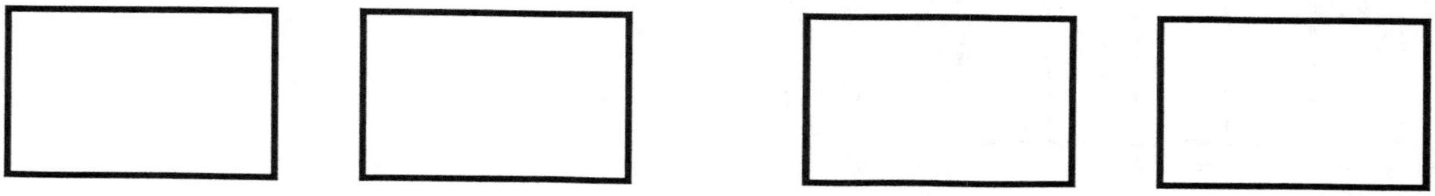

Focus on Fractions, Book 1 © 1977, 1987 Activity Resources Co., Inc. PO Box 4875, Hayward, CA 94540

MIXED NUMBERS AND IMPROPER FRACTIONS

Each picture has been divided into _____

Write an improper fraction for the halves

that are shaded. _____

Write a mixed number. _____

Each picture has been divided into _____

Write an improper fraction for the sixths

that are shaded. _____

Write a mixed number. _____

Each picture has been divided into _____

Write an improper fraction for the shaded

parts. _____

Write a mixed number. _____

Each picture has been divided into _____

Write an improper fraction for the shaded

parts _____

Write a mixed number. _____

Focus on Fractions, Book 1 © 1977, 1987 Activity Resources Co., Inc. PO Box 4875, Hayward, CA 94540

CHANGING IMPROPER FRACTIONS TO MIXED NUMBERS

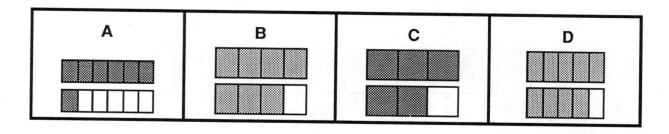

A	B	C	D

Write an improper fraction for picture A. ___ Did you write 7/6? ___
To write a mixed number for 7/6, think of 7/6 as the division 7 ÷ 6.

$$
\begin{array}{r}
1 \quad 1/6 \\
6\overline{)7} \\
\underline{6} \\
1
\end{array}
$$

Write an improper fraction for picture B. ___ Did you write 7/4? ___
To write a mixed number for 7/4, think of 7/4 as the division 7 ÷ 4.

$$
\begin{array}{r}
1 \quad 3/4 \\
4\overline{)7} \\
\underline{4} \\
3
\end{array}
$$

Write improper fractions for pictures C and D. Change the improper fractions to mixed numbers by using the division method.

PICTURE C

PICTURE D

Change these improper fractions to mixed or whole numbers.

$\dfrac{7}{2}$ =　　　$\dfrac{12}{4}$ =　　　$\dfrac{15}{6}$ =　　　$\dfrac{4}{4}$ =　　　$\dfrac{20}{8}$ =

$\dfrac{8}{4}$ =　　　$\dfrac{18}{8}$ =　　　$\dfrac{14}{9}$ =　　　$\dfrac{14}{4}$ =　　　$\dfrac{60}{11}$ =

Focus on Fractions, Book 1 © 1977, 1987 Activity Resources Co., Inc. PO Box 4875, Hayward, CA 94540

CHANGING A MIXED NUMBER TO AN IMPROPER FRACTION

Complete the following.

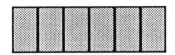 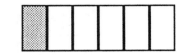

$1\dfrac{1}{6}$ =   6 sixths   +   ___ sixth   =   ___ sixths = 7/6

$$1\dfrac{1}{6} = \dfrac{7}{6}$$

 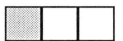

2 2/3 =   ___ thirds   +   ___ thirds   +   ___ thirds   = ___ thirds =

$$2\dfrac{2}{3} = \dfrac{}{3}$$

2 4/5 =   ___ fifths   +   ___ fifths   +   ___ fifths   = ___ fifths =

$$\dfrac{4}{5} = \dfrac{}{5}$$

Short cut:

$$4\dfrac{1}{3} = \dfrac{(4 \times 3) + 1}{3} \qquad \dfrac{13}{3}$$

$$7\dfrac{2}{9} = \dfrac{(7 \times 9) + 2}{9} \qquad \dfrac{}{9}$$

Try these:

$4\dfrac{3}{8} =$ $8\dfrac{3}{7} =$ $4\dfrac{2}{4} =$ $2\dfrac{2}{3} =$

$7\dfrac{2}{6} =$ $3\dfrac{5}{8} =$ $5\dfrac{4}{5} =$ $9\dfrac{5}{11} =$

$1\dfrac{7}{12} =$ $3\dfrac{5}{6} =$ $6\dfrac{2}{10} =$ $4\dfrac{2}{9} =$

LET'S REVIEW

LOWEST TERMS

Reduce these fractions to lowest terms.

$\dfrac{5}{15} = \dfrac{1}{3}$ $\qquad$ $\dfrac{7}{21} = $ ___ $\qquad$ $\dfrac{3}{12} = $ ___ $\qquad$ $\dfrac{7}{35} = $ ___

$\dfrac{9}{15} = $ ___ $\qquad$ $\dfrac{5}{10} = $ ___ $\qquad$ $\dfrac{8}{12} = $ ___ $\qquad$ $\dfrac{10}{20} = $ ___

$\dfrac{12}{24} = $ ___ $\qquad$ $\dfrac{8}{24} = $ ___ $\qquad$ $\dfrac{10}{40} = $ ___ $\qquad$ $\dfrac{16}{18} = $ ___

IMPROPER FRACTIONS

Change these improper fractions to mixed numbers.

$\dfrac{3}{2} = 1\,\dfrac{1}{2}$ $\qquad$ $\dfrac{7}{5} = $ $\qquad$ $\dfrac{7}{3} = $ $\qquad$ $\dfrac{12}{5} = $

$\dfrac{13}{4} = $ $\qquad$ $\dfrac{6}{5} = $ $\qquad$ $\dfrac{10}{8} = $ $\qquad$ $\dfrac{7}{2} = $

$\dfrac{12}{6} = $ $\qquad$ $\dfrac{16}{3} = $ $\qquad$ $\dfrac{5}{2} = $ $\qquad$ $\dfrac{9}{4} = $

MIXED NUMBERS

Change these mixed numbers to improper fractions.

$2\,\dfrac{4}{5} = \dfrac{14}{5}$ $\qquad$ $6\,\dfrac{2}{3} = $ $\qquad$ $7\,\dfrac{3}{4} = $ $\qquad$ $3\,\dfrac{2}{11} = $

$6\,\dfrac{3}{5} = $ $\qquad$ $4\,\dfrac{3}{8} = $ $\qquad$ $7\,\dfrac{2}{5} = $ $\qquad$ $5\,\dfrac{6}{7} = $

(Take Quiz 4)

Focus on Fractions, Book 1 © 1977, 1987 Activity Resources Co., Inc. PO Box 4875, Hayward, CA 94540

PUZZLE PAGE

Change all of the improper fractions to mixed numbers.
Trace a path through the maze moving to the largest number possible.

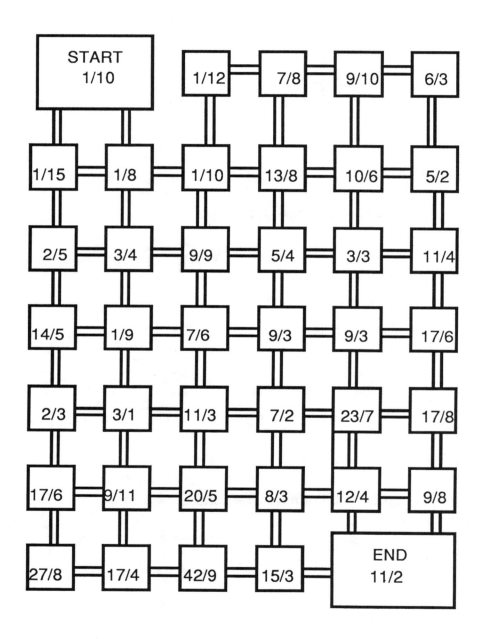

ADDING LIKE FRACTIONS

Fill in the blanks.

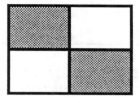 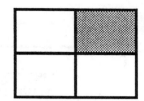 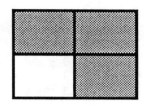

___ fourths   +   ___ fourth   =   ___ fourths

3 sixths + 2 sixths = _____ sixths

2 fifths + 1 fifth = _____ fifths

2 tenths + 5 tenths = _____ tenths

7 twelfths + 3 twelfths = _____ twelfths

3 fourteenths + 10 fourteenths = _____ fourteenths

Fill in the missing numerators.

$\dfrac{2}{12} + \dfrac{3}{12} = \dfrac{}{12}$ $\dfrac{7}{10} + \dfrac{2}{10} = \dfrac{}{10}$ $\dfrac{4}{11} + \dfrac{5}{11} = \dfrac{}{11}$

$\dfrac{2}{5} + \dfrac{2}{5} = \dfrac{}{5}$ $\dfrac{2}{13} + \dfrac{4}{13} = \dfrac{}{13}$ $\dfrac{3}{9} + \dfrac{4}{9} = \dfrac{}{9}$

$\dfrac{3}{14} + \dfrac{8}{14} = \dfrac{}{14}$ $\dfrac{2}{6} + \dfrac{3}{6} = \dfrac{}{6}$ $\dfrac{3}{8} + \dfrac{2}{8} = \dfrac{}{8}$

Add these fractions.

$\dfrac{3}{12} + \dfrac{5}{12} = \dfrac{}{}$ $\dfrac{4}{10} + \dfrac{3}{10} = \dfrac{}{}$ $\dfrac{3}{11} + \dfrac{2}{11} = \dfrac{}{}$

$\dfrac{1}{5} + \dfrac{2}{5} = \dfrac{}{}$ $\dfrac{1}{13} + \dfrac{5}{13} = \dfrac{}{}$ $\dfrac{2}{9} + \dfrac{5}{9} = \dfrac{}{}$

Focus on Fractions, Book 1 © 1977, 1987 Activity Resources Co., Inc. PO Box 4875, Hayward, CA 94540

ADDING LIKE FRACTIONS

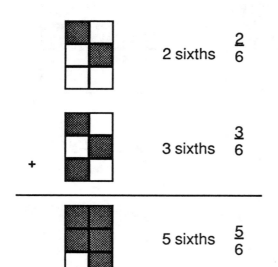

2 sixths $\dfrac{2}{6}$

+

3 sixths $\dfrac{3}{6}$

5 sixths $\dfrac{5}{6}$

LIKE FRACTIONS ARE FRACTIONS THAT HAVE THE SAME DENOMINATOR.

TO ADD LIKE FRACTIONS:

1. ADD THE NUMERATORS.

2. KEEP THE SAME DENOMINATORS.

3. REDUCE ANSWER TO LOWEST TERMS

Add the numerators of these fractions to find each sum. Reduce answers to lowest terms.

$\dfrac{2}{5}$	$\dfrac{3}{8}$	$\dfrac{5}{6}$	$\dfrac{3}{4}$	$\dfrac{2}{5}$
$+\ \dfrac{1}{5}$	$\dfrac{1}{8}$	$\dfrac{2}{6}$	$\dfrac{1}{4}$	$\dfrac{4}{5}$
$\dfrac{3}{5}$				

$\dfrac{6}{7}$	$\dfrac{5}{8}$	$\dfrac{2}{3}$	$\dfrac{4}{9}$	$\dfrac{7}{8}$
$+\ \dfrac{5}{7}$	$\dfrac{7}{8}$	$\dfrac{1}{3}$	$\dfrac{5}{9}$	$\dfrac{3}{8}$

$\dfrac{3}{4}$	$\dfrac{6}{9}$	$\dfrac{4}{8}$	$\dfrac{9}{2}$	$\dfrac{4}{5}$
$+\ \dfrac{5}{4}$	$\dfrac{5}{9}$	$\dfrac{7}{8}$	$\dfrac{3}{2}$	$\dfrac{6}{5}$

Focus on Fractions, Book 1 © 1977, 1987 Activity Resources Co., Inc. PO Box 4875, Hayward, CA 94540

ADDING THREE LIKE FRACTIONS

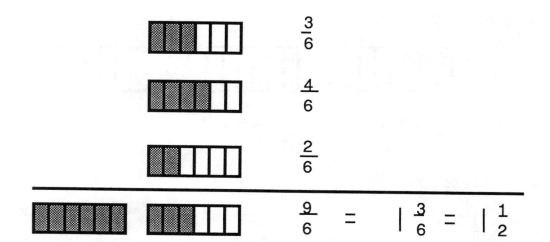

$$\frac{3}{6}$$

$$\frac{4}{6}$$

$$\frac{2}{6}$$

$$\frac{9}{6} \; = \; |\frac{3}{6} \; = \; |\frac{1}{2}$$

Add and reduce to lowest terms.

$$\begin{array}{r}\frac{3}{10}\\[4pt]\frac{2}{10}\\[4pt]+\frac{5}{10}\\\hline\end{array}\qquad\begin{array}{r}\frac{7}{8}\\[4pt]\frac{9}{8}\\[4pt]+\frac{1}{8}\\\hline\end{array}\qquad\begin{array}{r}\frac{7}{6}\\[4pt]\frac{11}{6}\\[4pt]+\frac{3}{6}\\\hline\end{array}\qquad\begin{array}{r}\frac{5}{18}\\[4pt]\frac{4}{18}\\[4pt]+\frac{15}{18}\\\hline\end{array}\qquad\begin{array}{r}\frac{5}{6}\\[4pt]\frac{7}{6}\\[4pt]+\frac{3}{6}\\\hline\end{array}$$

$$\begin{array}{r}\frac{3}{5}\\[4pt]\frac{3}{5}\\[4pt]+\frac{3}{5}\\\hline\end{array}\qquad\begin{array}{r}\frac{7}{8}\\[4pt]\frac{7}{8}\\[4pt]+\frac{11}{8}\\\hline\end{array}\qquad\begin{array}{r}\frac{6}{2}\\[4pt]\frac{1}{2}\\[4pt]+\frac{1}{2}\\\hline\end{array}\qquad\begin{array}{r}\frac{5}{12}\\[4pt]\frac{9}{12}\\[4pt]+\frac{6}{12}\\\hline\end{array}\qquad\begin{array}{r}\frac{1}{8}\\[4pt]\frac{1}{8}\\[4pt]+\frac{1}{8}\\\hline\end{array}$$

Focus on Fractions, Book 1 © 1977, 1987 Activity Resources Co., Inc. PO Box 4875, Hayward, CA 94540

SUBTRACTING LIKE FRACTIONS

Fill in the blanks.

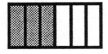   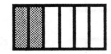   

___ sixths   -   ___ sixths   =   ___ sixths

Fill in the missing numerators.

$$\frac{3}{5} - \frac{1}{5} = \frac{}{5}$$ $$\frac{2}{3} - \frac{1}{3} = \frac{}{3}$$ $$\frac{11}{16} - \frac{4}{16} = \frac{}{16}$$

$$\frac{5}{7} - \frac{1}{7} = \frac{}{7}$$ $$\frac{5}{9} - \frac{2}{9} = \frac{}{9}$$ $$\frac{12}{12} - \frac{7}{12} = \frac{}{12}$$

Subtract and reduce to lowest terms.

$$\frac{7}{8} - \frac{3}{8} = \underline{\quad}$$ $$\frac{7}{12} - \frac{4}{12} = \underline{\quad}$$ $$\frac{9}{2} - \frac{8}{2} = \underline{\quad}$$

$$\frac{5}{2} - \frac{1}{2} = \underline{\quad}$$ $$\frac{4}{18} - \frac{2}{18} = \underline{\quad}$$ $$\frac{9}{12} - \frac{1}{12} = \underline{\quad}$$

Subtract the numerators to find each difference. Reduce answers to lowest terms.

$$\frac{15}{18} - \frac{3}{18}$$ $$\frac{3}{4} - \frac{1}{4}$$ $$\frac{8}{10} - \frac{2}{10}$$ $$\frac{7}{14} - \frac{3}{14}$$

$$\frac{15}{18} - \frac{12}{18}$$ $$\frac{9}{30} - \frac{6}{30}$$ $$\frac{16}{20} - \frac{10}{20}$$ $$\frac{21}{27} - \frac{12}{27}$$

(Take Quiz 5)

Focus on Fractions, Book 1 © 1977, 1987 Activity Resources Co., Inc. PO Box 4875, Hayward, CA 94540

NAME: _____

QUIZ 1

Write a fraction for the shaded part of each picture.

___   ___   ___   ___

In the fraction 4/5, the numerator is _____.

In the fraction 1/3, the denominator is _____

In the fraction 8/9, the denominator is _____

In the fraction 3/5, the numerator is _____

Shade 2/3 of this group.   Shade 4/5 of this group.

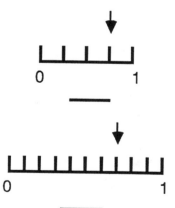   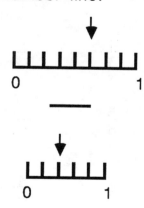

Write the fraction indicated by the arrow on each number line.

___

___

___   ___

QUIZ 2

Use the symbols < or > to compare the first fraction picture with the second.

            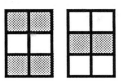

——   ——   ——

Insert the missing numerator so that each pair of fractions will be equivalent.

$$\frac{1}{3} = \frac{}{9} \qquad \frac{2}{3} = \frac{}{6} \qquad \frac{3}{4} = \frac{}{12} \qquad \frac{1}{5} = \frac{}{15}$$

$$\frac{5}{6} = \frac{}{18} \qquad \frac{2}{3} = \frac{}{18} \qquad \frac{7}{8} = \frac{}{16} \qquad \frac{1}{9} = \frac{}{72}$$

$$\frac{5}{8} = \frac{}{40} \qquad \frac{2}{5} = \frac{}{25} \qquad \frac{7}{8} = \frac{}{24} \qquad \frac{5}{6} = \frac{}{30}$$

Write the next three fractions in each series.

$$\frac{1}{6} \qquad \frac{2}{12} \qquad \frac{3}{18} \qquad \text{——} \qquad \text{——} \qquad \text{——}$$

$$\frac{5}{6} \qquad \frac{10}{12} \qquad \frac{15}{18} \qquad \text{——} \qquad \text{——} \qquad \text{——}$$

$$\frac{2}{7} \qquad \frac{4}{14} \qquad \frac{6}{21} \qquad \text{——} \qquad \text{——} \qquad \text{——}$$

$$\frac{1}{10} \qquad \frac{2}{20} \qquad \frac{3}{30} \qquad \text{——} \qquad \text{——} \qquad \text{——}$$

QUIZ 3

Write the next three fractions in each series.

$\dfrac{3}{8}$ $\dfrac{6}{16}$ $\dfrac{9}{24}$ ___ ___ ___

$\dfrac{4}{3}$ $\dfrac{8}{6}$ $\dfrac{12}{9}$ ___ ___ ___

$\dfrac{4}{11}$ $\dfrac{8}{22}$ $\dfrac{12}{33}$ ___ ___ ___

A fraction is in lowest terms if it cannot be re_____.

Reduce these fractions to lowest terms.

$\dfrac{6}{8} =$ $\dfrac{15}{18} =$ $\dfrac{6}{16} =$ $\dfrac{5}{25} =$ $\dfrac{2}{8} =$

$\dfrac{4}{6} =$ $\dfrac{8}{12} =$ $\dfrac{16}{48} =$ $\dfrac{12}{36} =$ $\dfrac{9}{36} =$

$\dfrac{9}{18} =$ $\dfrac{9}{27} =$ $\dfrac{8}{32} =$ $\dfrac{8}{10} =$ $\dfrac{12}{16} =$

Insert the missing numerator or denominator so that each pair of fractions will be equivalent.

$\dfrac{2}{11} = \dfrac{}{44}$ $\dfrac{2}{5} = \dfrac{}{20}$ $\dfrac{3}{4} = \dfrac{9}{}$ $\dfrac{5}{6} = \dfrac{30}{}$

$\dfrac{3}{7} = \dfrac{}{21}$ $\dfrac{1}{3} = \dfrac{5}{}$ $\dfrac{2}{9} = \dfrac{8}{}$ $\dfrac{1}{2} = \dfrac{}{18}$

$\dfrac{2}{3} = \dfrac{8}{}$ $\dfrac{3}{8} = \dfrac{}{24}$ $\dfrac{3}{10} = \dfrac{}{30}$ $\dfrac{5}{12} = \dfrac{}{36}$

QUIZ 4

Write a mixed number or a whole number for each improper fraction. Reduce answers to lowest terms.

$\dfrac{10}{4}$ = $\dfrac{15}{3}$ = $\dfrac{8}{3}$ = $\dfrac{12}{9}$ = $\dfrac{12}{12}$ =

$\dfrac{11}{5}$ = $\dfrac{23}{7}$ = $\dfrac{40}{12}$ = $\dfrac{18}{4}$ = $\dfrac{24}{16}$ =

$\dfrac{18}{12}$ = $\dfrac{15}{10}$ = $\dfrac{49}{6}$ = $\dfrac{20}{6}$ = $\dfrac{11}{8}$ =

Write an improper fraction for each mixed number.

2 4/5 =   6 1/3 =   2 3/8 =   4 1/2 =

3 2/3 =   5 4/5 =   7 2/6 =   8 4/5 =

2 3/9 =   1 5/6 =   6 2/7 =   4 1/3 =

Reduce these fractions to lowest terms.

$\dfrac{15}{20}$ = $\dfrac{14}{28}$ = $\dfrac{3}{9}$ = $\dfrac{2}{14}$ =

$\dfrac{18}{32}$ = $\dfrac{9}{15}$ = $\dfrac{6}{9}$ = $\dfrac{15}{33}$ =

$\dfrac{20}{24}$ = $\dfrac{7}{28}$ = $\dfrac{6}{8}$ = $\dfrac{8}{12}$ =

Focus on Fractions, Book 1 © 1977, 1987 Activity Resources Co., Inc. PO Box 4875, Hayward, CA 94540

QUIZ 5

Add these like fractions and reduce answers to lowest terms.

$$\frac{1}{12}$$ $$\frac{2}{5}$$ $$\frac{6}{8}$$ $$\frac{8}{10}$$

$$+\ \frac{9}{12}$$ $$+\ \frac{7}{5}$$ $$+\ \frac{4}{8}$$ $$+\ \frac{9}{10}$$

—   —   —   —

$$\frac{2}{7}$$ $$\frac{3}{20}$$ $$\frac{4}{9}$$ $$\frac{2}{8}$$

$$\frac{4}{7}$$ $$\frac{14}{20}$$ $$\frac{6}{9}$$ $$\frac{6}{8}$$

$$+\ \frac{3}{7}$$ $$+\ \frac{6}{20}$$ $$+\ \frac{5}{9}$$ $$+\ \frac{9}{8}$$

—   —   —   —

Subtract these like fractions and reduce answers to lowest terms.

$$\frac{14}{15}$$ $$\frac{12}{12}$$ $$\frac{20}{28}$$ $$\frac{16}{18}$$

$$-\ \frac{8}{15}$$ $$-\ \frac{8}{12}$$ $$-\ \frac{14}{28}$$ $$-\ \frac{12}{18}$$

$$\frac{22}{100}$$ $$\frac{25}{50}$$ $$\frac{14}{16}$$ $$\frac{12}{25}$$

$$-\ \frac{12}{100}$$ $$-\ \frac{15}{50}$$ $$-\ \frac{5}{16}$$ $$-\ \frac{7}{25}$$

ANSWERS

PAGE 4

ANSWERS WILL VARY.

PAGE 5

3/9   1/2   2/5

PAGE 6

3/4   4/8   5/12

PAGE 7

2
3
NUMERATOR
DENOMINATOR
5/7
5/9
BOTTOM
TOP
SIX
ONE
FOUR
FIVE TWELFTHS
ONE FOURTH
NINE TENTHS
THREE EIGHTHS

PAGE 8

YOU NAME IT

PAGE 9

ANSWERS WILL VARY

PAGE 10

ANSWERS WILL VARY

PAGE 11

ANSWERS WILL VARY

PAGE 12

1/3   2/4   6/10   6/10

PAGE 13

WHOLE

5/6   2/8   5/9

3	7	9	4	15	2
4	8	16	5	16	3

12 SQUARES   9 CIRCLES

9/10   1/3

PAGE 14

YOU'RE DONE

PAGE 15

3/6 > 2/6   3/5 > 2/5

1/2 = 1/2   1/4 < 2/4

3/10 > 1/10

PAGE 16

1/3 > 1/4   1/4 < 1/2

1/4 < 3/8   2/4 < 5/8

3/6 = 1/2

PAGE 17

FRACTION

Focus on Fractions, Book 1 © 1977, 1987 Activity Resources Co., Inc. PO Box 4875, Hayward, CA 94540

PAGE 18

	7/7	9/9
2/2	3/3	5/5
3/3	5/5	8/8

PAGE 19

18	7	16
10	4	10
6	20	10
9	10	6
6	10	30
7	21	12

PAGE 20

1/2 2/4 3/6 4/8 5/10 6/12 7/14 8/16
1/3 2/6 3/9 4/12 5/15 6/18 7/21 8/24
2/3 4/6 6/9 8/12 10/15 12/18 14/21 16/24
1/4 2/8 3/12 4/16 5/20 6/24 7/28 8/32
3/4 6/8 9/12 12/16 15/20 18/24 21/28 24/32
1/5 2/10 3/15 4/20 5/25 6/30 7/35 8/40
2/5 4/10 6/15 8/20 10/25 12/30 14/35 16/40
3/5 6/10 9/15 12/20 15/25 18/30 21/35 24/40
1/6 2/12 3/18 4/24 5/30 6/36 7/42 8/48
5/6 10/12 15/18 20/24 25/30 30/36 35/42 40/48

PAGE 21

2/3 4/5

9	3	25	28	6
56	40	25	49	77
36	44	81	25	63
=	≠	≠	≠	=
≠	=	≠	=	≠
≠	=	≠	≠	≠

PAGE 22

YOU ARE ALMOST THROUGH

PAGE 23

3/6

7/14 8/16

LOWER TERMS			HIGHER TERMS	
1/4	2/8	3/12	5/20	6/24
2/5	4/10 6/15	8/20	12/30	

PAGE 24

1/2	3/4	2/3
1/3	3/8	2/6
4/6	2/3	1/3
2/6	2/6	2/4

Focus on Fractions, Book 1 © 1977, 1987 Activity Resources Co., Inc. PO Box 4875, Hayward, CA 94540

PAGE 25

	1/2	1/4
3/4	1/2	1/8
2/3	2/3	1/3
1/3	1/4	2/5
3/8	3/5	2/5

PAGE 26

10/15 12/18 14/21

10/35 12/42 14/49

15/25 18/30 21/35

9	10	12	6
30	18	6	24
8	9	16	20
1/2	1/3	1/8	1/6
1/5	1/10	1/6	5/8
2/5	3/4	2/3	1/10

PAGE 27

THE SHADED PART WILL REVEAL
A PATTERN

PAGE 28

1/4   2/2   2/5   4/4

YES
YES
YES
YES

8/5   9/4   6/3   9/9   7/7
Answers will vary.

PAGE 29

5 3/4   4 7/8   6 2/3

FOURTHS	5	
HALVES	5	
	5/2	2 1/2

PAGE 30

HALVES	3/2	1 1/2
SIXTHS	13/6	2 1/6
FOURTHS	2 1/4	5 1/4
FIFTHS	6/5	1 1/5

PAGE 31

C =	5/3	1 2/3		
D =	9/5	1 4/5		
3 1/2	3	2 1/2	1	2 1/2
2	2 1/4	1 5/9	3 1/2	5 5/11

PAGE 32

35/8	59/7	18/4	8/3
44/6	29/8	29/5	104/11
19/12	23/6	62/10	38/9

PAGE 33

	1/3	1/4	1/5
3/5	1/2	2/3	1/2
1/2	1/3	1/4	8/9
	1 2/5	2 1/3	2 2/5
3 1/4	1 1/5	1 1/4	3 1/2
2	5 1/3	2 1/2	2 1/4
	20/3	31/4	35/11
33/5	35/8	37/5	41/7

PAGE 35

	2	1	3
		5	
		3	
		7	

Focus on Fractions, Book 1 © 1977, 1987 Activity Resources Co., Inc. PO Box 4875, Hayward, CA 94540

PAGE 35

$$\frac{10}{13}$$

5	9	9
4	6	7
11	5	5

$$\frac{2}{3} \quad \frac{7}{10} \quad \frac{5}{11}$$

$$\frac{3}{5} \quad \frac{6}{13} \quad \frac{7}{9}$$

PAGE 36

1/2   1 1/6   1   1 1/5

1 1/2   1   1   1 1/4

2   1 2/9   1 3/8   6   2

PAGE 37

1   2 1/8   3 1/2   1 1/3   2 1/2

1 4/5   3 1/8`   4   1 2/3   3/8

PAGE 38

3	2	1
2	1	7
4	3	5

$$\frac{1}{2} \quad \frac{1}{4} \quad \frac{1}{2}$$

$$2 \quad \frac{1}{9} \quad \frac{2}{3}$$

$$\frac{1}{2} \quad \frac{3}{5} \quad \frac{2}{7}$$

$$\frac{1}{6} \quad \frac{1}{10} \quad \frac{3}{10} \quad \frac{1}{3}$$

QUIZ 1

3/8   2/5   6/12   1/6

$$4$$
$$3$$
$$9$$
$$3$$

8 SQUARES SHADED ,   8 CIRCLES SHADED

3/4   5/8
7/10   2/5

QUIZ 2

<	>	>	
3	4	9	3
15	12	14	8
25	10	21	25

$$\frac{4}{24} \quad \frac{5}{30} \quad \frac{6}{36}$$

$$\frac{20}{24} \quad \frac{25}{30} \quad \frac{30}{36}$$

$$\frac{8}{28} \quad \frac{10}{35} \quad \frac{12}{42}$$

$$\frac{4}{40} \quad \frac{5}{50} \quad \frac{6}{60}$$

QUIZ 3

$$\frac{12}{32} \quad \frac{15}{40} \quad \frac{18}{48}$$

$$\frac{16}{12} \quad \frac{20}{15} \quad \frac{24}{18}$$

$$\frac{16}{44} \quad \frac{20}{55} \quad \frac{24}{66}$$

$$\frac{3}{4} \quad \frac{5}{6} \quad \frac{3}{8} \quad \frac{1}{5} \quad \frac{1}{4}$$

$$\frac{2}{3} \quad \frac{2}{3} \quad \frac{1}{3} \quad \frac{1}{3} \quad \frac{1}{4}$$

Focus on Fractions, Book 1 © 1977, 1987 Activity Resources Co., Inc. PO Box 4875, Hayward, CA 94540

QUIZ 3 (CONT)

1/2	1/3	1/4	4/5	3/4
	8	8	12	36
	12	9	9	15

QUIZ 4

2 1/2	5	2 2/3	1 1/3	1
2 1/5	3 2/7	3 1/3	4 1/2	1 1/2
1 1/2	1 1/2	8 1/6	3 1/3	1 3/8
14/5	19/3	19/8	9/2	
11/3	29/5	44/6	44/5	
21/9	16/11	44/7	13/3	
3/4	1/2	1/3	1/7	
9/16	3/5	2/3	5/11	
5/6	1/4	3/4	2/3	

QUIZ 5

5/6	1 4/5	1 1/4	1 7/10
1 2/7	1 3/20	1 2/3	2 1/8
2/5	1/3	3/14	2/9
1/10	1/5	9/16	1/5

Focus on Fractions, Book 1 © 1977, 1987 Activity Resources Co., Inc. PO Box 4875, Hayward, CA 94540